*Dedicated to all of my students through the years,
big and small...*

With gratitude to my family, friends, and colleagues for their love, kindness, and support.

Printed in the United States of America
First Printing, 2024
ISBN 979-8-9890108-2-0
Earth and Elements Publishing
New York
www.earthandelementspublishing.com

Silly House
of
ABCs
Written by Lory Reed
Art by Nicolas de Leon, Jr.

One silly night,
In my big silly house,
I heard some silly noises,
Some footsteps and some voices.
ABC
Clang!
Maa!
Clink!
Stomp!
Squish!

So, I went out of my bedroom,
And walked around every nook.
I saw silly ABCs,
And I curiously took a look.
Honk!
Roar!
Clank!
Growl!
Ooo!
Aa Bb Cc

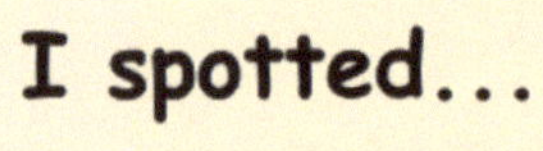

I spotted...
A for alligators,
Acting in the attic.
Aa

B for bears,
Bowling in the basement.
Bb

C for camels,
Camping in the closet.

Dd

E for elephants,
Entering everywhere.

Ee

F for flamingo,
Flying over the fan.
Ff

G for goat,
Grabbing some green grapes.

Gg

H for hippopotamus,
Holding a hairy hat.
Hh

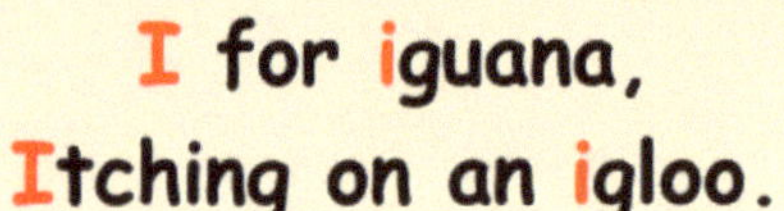

I for iguana,
Itching on an igloo.

Ii

Jj

K for kangaroo,
Kicking kiwis in the kitchen.
Kk

L for lobster,
Lighting up a lantern.
Ll

Mm

M for monkey,
Making a muddy mess.

N for newt,
Nibbling on nachos.
Nn
NACHOS

O for octopus,
Operating the oven.

P for peacock,
Polishing the pan.
Pp

Qq

R for racoon,
Running with a red ring.

Rr

Ss

T for tiger,
Tasting tacos at the table.

Uu

U for umbrellabird,
Under the umbrella.

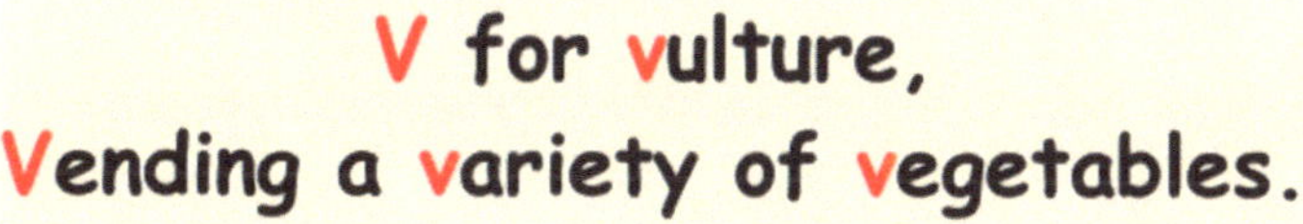

V for vulture,
Vending a variety of vegetables.

Vv

Ww

X for x-ray fish,
Exiting a box.
Xx

Yy
Y for yak,
Yanking a yellow yoyo.

Z for zebra,
Zipping up a zazzy zipper.
Zz

Suddenly,
I heard a loud "Bleep!".
I woke up from my sleep!
Bleep!

I realized that I was dreaming.
I fell asleep while I was playing!

It's fun to have such toys as these.
They make a silly house of ABCs!

Silly ABCs are everywhere!
Can you name each letter?
In the story,
What is the silly thing that each animal does?
Or, tell me,
What is the silly thing that each animal has?
Aa
Bb
Cc
Dd
Ee
Ff
Gg
Hh
Ii
Jj
Kk
Ll
Mm
Nn
Oo
Pp
Qq
Rr
Ss
Tt
Uu
Vv
Ww
Xx
Yy
Zz

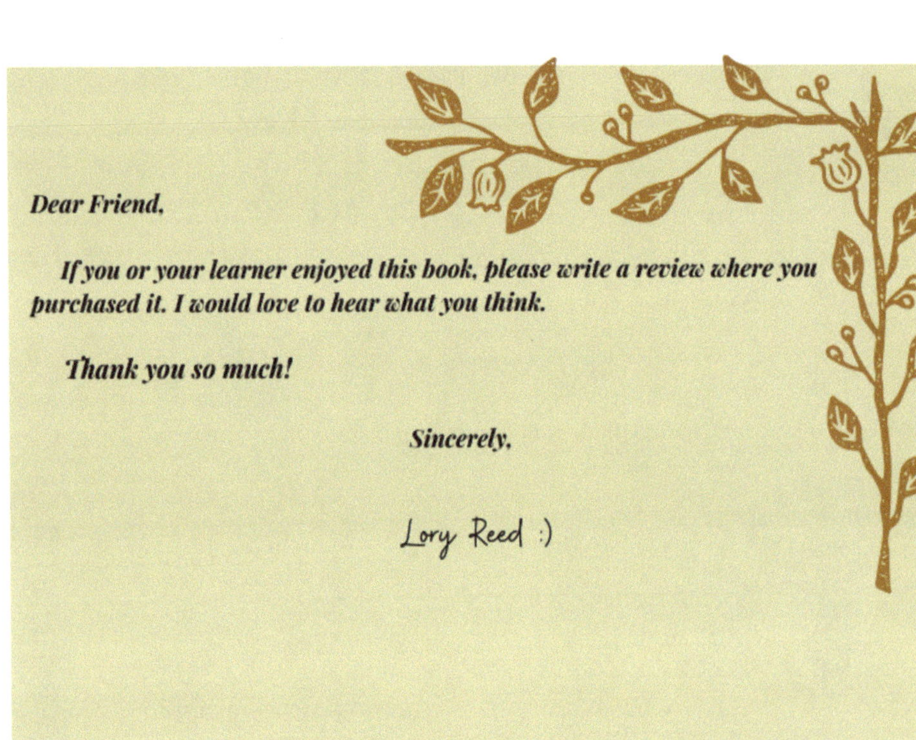

Dear Friend,

If you or your learner enjoyed this book, please write a review where you purchased it. I would love to hear what you think.

Thank you so much!

Sincerely,

Lory Reed :)

The Silly Learning Book Series

As a special education teacher and a Board Certified Behavior Analyst (BCBA), author Lory Reed often "pairs" her instruction with novelty (e.g., something new, funny, outrageous, etc.) which helps reinforce her students' positive learning responses and memory skills. Young learners generally love being silly, and that Lory believes that we should give them "something silly" added to their reading materials. Well, why not?

Get all the "Silly Learning" Titles!